From Hepworth's Garden

Out...

From Hepworth's Garden Out

edited by

Rupert Loydell

Shearsman Books
Exeter

First published in the United Kingdom in 2010 by
Shearsman Books Ltd
58 Velwell Road
Exeter EX4 4LD

www.shearsman.com

ISBN 978-1-84861-124-5
First Edition

CONTENTS

From Hepworth's Garden . . .

. . . Out

From Hepworth's Garden . . .

FROM HEPWORTH'S GARDEN OUT

In the dream (2008)

my father lives in the small town made famous by the painter
who once lived there. While he goes shopping for food, the rain
becomes torrential and floods the inside of the door, dampening
the drapes, and under it a pool spreads across the varnished
floorboards and collects between them. Later, in company,
the talk turns to art. One man speaks of the painter, uses the
word 'crèpelle', but I don't know what it means, though I feel
I ought. But when he comes to collect nibbles from the coffee
table, I notice the bottoms of his trousers curl round his shoes
like elephant trunks, empty sleeves, sodden from the rain. Open
on the table is a large thick book. Peering closer I see that it
displays an alphabet designed by Eric Gill. I think it odd that on
the record player is Berio, whose music—tinkles interrupted by
crashing drums—ill-fits this ambience. Indeed, I am dressed in
clothes in the style of the painter. I take off my sandy overcoat,
with its fur collar, to reveal a jacket and waistcoat and trousers,
all in the same sand yellow with a hint of mustard, and thin red
stripes. The cut is distinctly Edwardian, something of Algernon
Moncrieff or Rupert Bear, but I feel perfectly at ease. I know I
ought to be able to wear them in everyday life, outside of the
prose I have now written.

In the garden (1981)

the woman plays bo-beep
between sculptures

like she does
in another poem

behold
the abandoned studio

a single light-bulb
hanging on a wire

like it might
in another's drawing

the untouched marble
aloof in fecundity

pregnant with itself
with unfinish

we pull at it our mass
pulling at its centre

but it won't budge
not even in this poem

where nearly anything
could happen

In the painting (1932)

the surfaces pile
like plates of space

obscuring one another
drawing apart as one looks

the shadow of the
queen's profile

spills like hair
onto the stepped planes beneath

the colours of winter pasture
rubbed and smeared

grazed but glazed
frames half-drape frames

one shows horizontal
alternations (a beach rug)

another the sea uncertain uneven
blue cut by live-wire sun-crests

and a shallow field of sprouting
bathers

the queen gathers
her own place but her crown

shifts off into scribble
on a smoky headland

space grows impatient
to lock image

to reconfigure its dominion—
the relief of flats

Robert Sheppard

Contexts

*For twenty-five years, walking through these streets, I have felt
through my feet the geological shape of the place . . . St Ives has
absolutely enraptured me.* —Barbara Hepworth

Trewyn. She'd passed it for years without knowing
what lay behind those twenty-foot granite-block walls,
believing that sculpture "grows in the open light"
just as language can germinate in contexts in which
there is no language. Nothing more natural, then,
than to plant her sculptures under the sky there
among the roses and deep subtropical green.
So now one might pass the same walls and not know
Makutu is in there, Apollo and Cantate Domine,
Corymb, Coré, Torso II, River Form,
Sea Form, forms within forms, figures for landscapes,
conversations with magic stones, some smooth
as boulders licked by the sea's innumerable tongues,
others rough as if weathered like inland menhir
and dolmen; and not know the roses had to go,
for they obstructed the sculpture being wheeled around
to be placed with an exactitude bordering on mathematics
by those judgemental eyes; and not know that this garden
at the back of her studio is bigger than it is,
overlooked as it is by the parish church, and signposted,
caught in a street-map mesh . . . Tregenna Hill,
St Eia Street, Fish Street, Street-an-Garrow, The Digey . . .
a naming that, far from shutting outsiders out,
seduces with a poetry of its own, signalling
the very soul of the town as unmistakably
as the tilts and edges of its many roofs,
the truth of the lie of its land, the cries of its gulls,
the smell of its landed fish, any of the bate
that lured the artists here—a soul palpable

yet elusive as an erotic ideal, touched
only to be pushed away by the hand of language.

James Turner

SCULPTURES IN THE GARDEN
OF BARBARA HEPWORTH

a spring and summer
place with dappled sunshine blown
through the leaves all day

she was here but now
is not it seems she made things
metal wood and stone

so many many
views around behind up through
look carefully   see

verdigris patina
around a polished eyehole
look through now look through

bamboo and yucca
frame a metal tete a tete
on a pale stone plinth

three oblong holes in
a low squat body perhaps
female perhaps not

a binocular
bronze sphere on a pedestal
on a stone diamond

shears with no handles
or cantate domino
as she would call it

against the white wall
are you a river lozenge
or a shapely pod

among the bamboo
a slim grooved shaft is flanked by
chunky metal cubes

and a shorter grey
blotchy column lurks through there
under spiky palms

a blade with two holes
a phallic arum lily
sheathed in bright bronze

the former palais
de danse once her studio
has a calendar

open at the page
for may the twentieth nineteen
seventy five when

smoke snuffed out pure light
from her eyes and her garden
where sculptures still stand

she is here somewhere
crunching the gravel alone
then is now   surely

Geoff Sutton

EMERGENT POEM FOR BARBARA HEPWORTH

Barb

              p orth

     ra   w

  ar   p

             p ort

         He w

     ra   p   t

          p o t

     ra   p

           worth

  r ar   e

    ar   t

Bar   e

B   e   rth

Barbara Hepworth

Philip Terry

SPACES

as   commas   layers of thought
a golem's fingers behind   signatures
selling formless roses   your demand for liberty
attracts punctures of quiet
engraved blue-grey

a moment is too much
side to side   impossible
to write clearly   stained leaves
sunlight on paving

towards an ocean
waiting   the next name not called

green shoots turn the pages
you leave between this

Nathan Thompson

In the Garden

1995

                smilesmiles

here Jo takes another photo as if improving the torso though
    my hand on hip just so   really to turn me solid bronze
        elbow akimbo   to capture to be king of
            my body his   the female form is it
              can it be that   long ago was he right
              fixing my limb   the nerve the cheek
              head stapled on   becoming monu
    —mental with green scars
    green Docs n   scratched across
                hatching   green shade and a
                mayfly   kick of hip into the
                day   light we were and

              (this is the plinth)
                wings they were and still are

2009

we were doing Art; uncomfortable, rigorous
I don't know how to interpret this now

being repeatedly stripped and remade
a softer thing with less going on upstairs

if I went back today the plants would speak
while the sculptures threw simple shadows

that verdigris tells me only how
I've drawn an old self in its colour

although I remember cupping my hand
to see into the shed where the tools lived;

the joy of such human work

Sandra Tappenden

REFLECTION

Like a cast piece
on the white shelf of a gallery
part burnished round
but opening into deep unfinished space

composed, replete
poised stillness of a weight
gathering attention to itself
out of the vacancy around

until each movement past it
seems a disturbance of the air—

so her brief words
hang in the silence, rounded
as a white stone
dropped into standing water

the layers quietly unfold
as ripples spreading from a centre
targeted with care

till even moving to make note of this
is an evasive tangent taken
to escape the gravity of prayer.

Tony Lucas

Some Irregularics for Barbara Hepworth

In pumice stones of Cornwall
White holes of space.
In greeny parks
Worldwide
Rain slides your stone
And sunlight bites
Your lonely, lonely vision.

In oxydised bronze
And weird steel
All the grief at life's
Strange twists and turns
Of soul-shape.

How we gape in galleries
And gardens, heart-filled
And bone-chiselled
By your vision:
Everyway aware
Of your involuntary *suttee*
In that studio
By the brine-bright
Earth-bottled sea
The day the stones were pocked
With black holes again.

William Oxley

A PASSING POEM IN FOUR WHOLES
on Barbara Hepworth's "Four Square (walk through)"

First Whole

They met by The Hepworth, rounded outside,
fire drill, all urgencies; a merry-making
pause in seasonal cycles, something in the air.

Gospel, spin, mass, small general food store.
It all falls in. Centrifugal culture eating
away at general relatives. What goes missing

in action? Slaves to the circles we set free,
unrestrained short plays by Beckett.
Spinning and scratching: parallels we draw.

Walk through, walk on through, walk
through, walk on through, walk
through, walk on through.

Second Whole

The loops to Euclid leave us doubtful,
though sunshine outflows all alignment.
Lounge of love, spring, a weather thing.

What other-sides the mirrors? Midnight?
Baptism? Shrine? Temple? No entry
point is straight-laced, bracelets.

The dancers have danced their varying circles.
They spin not at all. As still as blackbirds
 dumbstruck by an aberrant event.

Walk on through, walk through, walk
on through, walk through, walk
on through, walk through.

Third Whole

These constellations stacked, offset.
To bevel out spacetime. What? No contents?
Look again: look at the wiry birch branch.

Look at the concrete pillar. Look at the walkway,
brickwork, green green grass of home away
from home, yew hedge with its red

constellations, shadings of sky-blue.
Palettes. Crushing weight of lightlessness
made luminous, dazzling!

Casual, tense, supercilious, amorous,
quickstep, foxtrot, Leibniz Equivalence:
"If two distributions of fields

are related by a smooth
transformation, then they represent
the same physical systems . . ."

Walk through, walk on through, walk
through, walk on through, walk
through, walk on through.

Fourth Whole

We staged an *event* and all passed
through O O O and O, the square
sucked out space, high dimensional

box car traipse and tour, go nowhere
on a lazy afternoon, fashionable
and naff, book-bound *and* fantasising,

equations easy as speak-easy
cloud inhalation, fructification!
Out of a cell, out of darkest places

to sing unrestrained, larynx
and syrinx, larynx and syrinx,
hole to hole, hole to hole,

cross-hatched walk, brisk stroll,
O how quartets harmonise differing points
of an echo: eyes to the wall: open to all.

Walk on through, walk through, walk
on through, walk through, walk
on through, walk through.

John Kinsella

HER GARDEN MY LURE

        absences hole
her   your intent

        green metal curves
        grey stone hulks
incidental
        within
                   your
own burgeoning
gaps

  look through
suffer   vertigo   depth
        intoxication
sweet tangling in hedged
                     corners
bitter salt winds rime
leathered leaves

scent   musk-sodden

nostrils sting   flare
wide   delighted

        cold   cannot speak
            fingers ram
    pockets. Neoprene hems

        discomfort   too
       to touch

        high still space
lofty   presence

preternaturally thickened
eddying   dance
  strength gnarled   limbs:
    fire   not extinguished

wet stone and salt-sheared grass
beyond the boundary gate

        rain
      did not fall

filled with   potential
  desire
such torque gains traction
in   structures' sustenance

Ursula Hurley

TREWYN STUDIO
St. Ives, May 1983 (revised 2009)

In her garden
I walked, musing, through her strewn bones
in spring light—sheltered by tall trees
and the hillside behind me, facing cottages
above the bay's smooth water. A blackbird
trilled in the branches—green-gold voice,
above the wind's flash that smoothed young leaves
in her quiet garden. High above my shoulder,
through a hole in the porcelain sky, seeped sun.
My path circled, through grass darkened by shadow,
hooping through shrubs and flower-constellations
and the secrets of her littoral garden,
beached shells of another's mind.

Here, where her feet once moved, her thoughts lay smiling.
And within the shade of her living garden
I stopped, thoughtful, lost in her mind's landscape,
my nerves tangled, feeling along cool lawns.
Yet I touched no human.

Pure stone found me, instead. Forms beyond visibility
as if they were numinous. A telluric alphabet—
bone, chitin, the invincible. Indecipherable messages
that reduced to themselves only. And nothing flimsy
for interpretation. Whilst all around, greens jigged
and yellows boasted from them, I saw their symbols
pearl-smooth, marble-sheeny,
granite-hard. In her nowhere garden

as the hacked blackbird gleamed, quarried into song.

Norman Jope

In the Garden

I broke the back of a
statue, a curved thing
stained with air, in the
garden near the glass-
house. Turned my head
to follow the slope of it,
and the whole dynamic
of the piece collapsed
around me.

Erect, the glint of the
metal brought me back to
the position I was at when,
eager to shift, I lifted my
eye from the steel to the
drifting of dry light; from
a substance to a feeling.

Later, in a square shop
near the harbour I saw a
canvas leaning at the
door. It was a Lowry that
gleamed in the low sun
coming off the sea. The
colour in it reminded me
of the verdigris on the
statue in the garden
which I'd turned my head
from and broken the back of.

John Gimblett

SCULPTING FROM NATURE

The earth, measuring her years in billions,
makes our own epoch rather small
on any but the largest timeline.

These plants knew an earlier earth:
cycads, eucalypts, conifers.
They're not familiar
so I come upon them
seeing all plants differently.

An artist worked here
planting and tending
time travelling among them.

For such geometry as the world is made of.
What *is* this structure that is a plant?
Rooted in the dark of earth
waiting for the force of light,
whatever light is,
to reach down, even through the rock,
to draw it up to feed from water and our breath
in the presence of the all-enabling light.

Sally Crawford

THE GARDEN OF HER ART

It is early May, summer
just around the corner
with its heat of glowing shapes
I would take to a desert
island along with sculptures
to watch (a) the effect
of shape on space while (b) hearing
its perfect sound in heaven;
even though gardens actually grow
through likes and dislikes and fashions
of the light and of the flowers that bloom;
and even though too much is known
of the artist from a child
prodigy to blazing grave
through, of course, her genius:
how she composed entirely
in her head while stretching her hands
out in perfect fingers,
a single smoothness;
although we now know utterly
exceptional and unteachable
giftedness is as much myth
as the making of *a fairyland*
when grasses are simply struck by frost;
or only as clever as sculpting
a dead tree into life;
and even though a forger lied
that her ideas flowed best
and most abundantly
when she was entirely alone,
though she couldn't say how they came
to fire her soul with invention
except that it was in a dream;

and even though we know this to be
nothing less than invention,
we still prefer it to be true,
otherwise how could we describe it:
as if flowers blossomed secretly
and best in the darkness of a cave
like miracles creating
as they should create
with absolute perfection,
incomprehensibly;
forever and forever
in the garden of her art.

Geoffrey Godbert

IN HER SUN PORCH

palm upturned
tap the flaming flare
petal   skirt
a living cylinder
xylem and phloem
veins and cells and
mitochondria conspire
to yield not one
drop
purely folded
empty handed
endured
nectar sweetened
space and lack

hallucinogen
brugmansia sanguinea
angel(')s trumpet
flesh filled potential
scentless
static (breeze-glazed)
behind cracked glass
salt-pricked
roots reaching through
dust
the dander of decades
bound by stone borders
in bone china corsets:
so neatly bandaged

Ursula Hurley

Remarks to Stone and Bronze

*"Could I, at one and the same time, be the outside
as well as the form within?"*

Asperged light let into me,
my shut form, does not come out.

★

Walkthrough outscape crawlspace insight
mind's eye land's lie light box lookout.

★

Pierced liths: techno-dreamtime
standing stones, sky-catchers.

★

Walked or stood, something in me
unabates, infused with geometry.

★

Cyme thyrse raceme
umbel panicle capitulum

★

Or, matter's mirror: whatness
in its blazing notness.

*

Where forms converse, I enter;
am appraised as not-I, non-I.

*

Corymb coré cantate
corinthos contrapuntto

David Kennedy

Note: The epigraph is a quotation from Barbara Hepworth. The
fifth poem uses botanical terms for arrangements of flowers on a
stem. The final poem uses titles of Hepworth sculptures.

THE BARBARA HEPWORTH MUSEUM
(first visit to St Ives)

Dazzled
gulls caw
across surf's scuffle

Delight!
Images paint themselves
at every turn

"Down to the harbour"

•

    Fingers
point blue

Stony stares

You walked in white rooms
drinking marble and plaster
mouthing circles and threads

    gestures
carved spaces

•

Gardening

Garden in bloom:
        the rain cupped
            in bronze

Old cacti
    nature's echo
        stacked forms

You worked in white rooms

shaping a future
we hold up
to the light

your town
reflected in
a polished metal sea

Portholes, arches
    the curve
        of your arm

White room

Death mask

•

Milk walls
poured onto cobbles
stream towards

sea walls
thrust into line
harbouring

boats
peppering the view
bobbing at

buoys
oranges adrift
Strange fruit

•

Dimpled mass
    hold-all
hand-held

handled
    into shape
by rasp, file, blade

Turntables
in dust

Balance
experienced

A stonethrow
from silence

Rupert M Loydell

ST IVES CONJUNCTION
for Barbara Hepworth

In the garden the sun
falls on the stone
forms, shimmers on the bronze
like fire on one
anvil and altar. Lone
shadows are tons-

ured by light. Feeling flows
from surface and
context, cast and leaf's writ,
bites in thought, throws
St. Ives bay wave and sand,
ribbed Yorkshire grit,

whin, marble, Penwith rock
in the one furn-
ace, fired to affirma-
tion by the cock
of her mind, white-hot earn-
er of new sta-

tes of playing. Wakefield is
come to Trewyn:
Riding contours, Roman
skies are in kiss
of chisel on stone. In
whin's the woman.

Brian Louis Pearce

GARDEN WITH TORSO II

Am I Alcestis or Electra,
Dido or Eurydice
enchanted into *brons*,

the bar of my grief lifted,
moving me unmoving
through green brights, green dims?

I'm the pure reduction of a woman
in a garden of forms

dancing where we stand stock-still
amid the applause of foliage,

sisters to those wild petric maidens
who dance forever without stirring

on the high heathland beyond the town,
circled by gorse and *krann* and salt-woven air—

I'm the tall heartshaped pillar
more articulate than Lot's wife,
speaking through touch,

receiving a daily tribute of hands,
giving back my tactile answers—

All of me that is not figured,
head, limbs,
is drawn into my proud dark core,
where all ripens,

is implicit in the beautiful absences
of limb and head,
my sheernesses *leun a ras*—
my hollows cupping the light . . .

My brother, Light,
who stays with me so late into the evening,
can't get enough of my bronze poise,

the rooted *lowen* of my invisible arms
gathering the worthy and the unworthy to my breast—

Electra or Alcestis,
Dido, Eurydice or Everywoman . . .

Penelope Shuttle

Cornish Glossary:
brons—bronze
krann—scrub
leun a ras—full of grace
lowen—joy

Garden with Torso II, 1959
Bronze
Tate Gallery (T 03138)
Barbara Hepworth Museum and Sculpture Garden

AMONG SCULPTURE

Narrow streets lead to the same place
whichever way you take sea drawing up
on the sand breakers alive a solitary surfer
heads out benches at the harbour taped off

It is upon this unity that our continued existence depends

Twenty foot walled garden shaded from wind
battering a blue like no other blue edges the wall
fresh from the horizon matches the nature of
the garden to grow and change with the seasons

Our sense of touch is a fundamental sensibility

A place to worship daily where the wind
sneaks through gaps between Cornish Granite
off the sea where St Ia ended her lonely journey
and gave her name to a town

Finding Trewyn Studio was a sort of magic

hidden amongst narrow streets past a steamed
up tea shop sanctuary for out of season tourists
spending time in Hepworth's garden plant
spotting among the sculpture

Andrew Taylor

. . . Out

ENTERING LIGHT AT ST IVES

1.

Silence becoming light silence,
stone becoming the speech of light.

2.

Entering light that lifts
and what the mind will make of this
and what cannot be said cascading
into something only attempted.

3.

What we bring here falls back
because of perceptions and expectations
and what the mind insists upon.

4.

What the sea says when it meets the sky,
what the water makes of tides and time
and the gorse garlanding.

5.

I came here to be with others
and as I entered I was alone again
sand into sky into sun.

6.

The words on the grave tiles muttering
but I could not hear them because
of the words held in my heart.

7.

The light says yes and the silence says
listen to me and the music says if only
we had more time.

8.

What do we bring but the noises that have failed us?
What do we ever say but other people's riddles?
These stones reaching above our definitions of eternity.

9.

And is the God here, intent, listening?
Does He see us in our hauling of the holy,
does He care about our futures and fumbling,

does he go out into the shades of trees and listen
as our silences begin again, as we walk away and
drive back to our houses and careful constructions?

10.

The centre of the stone is moon,
in the healing, in the shaping, in the way of the idea;
the centre of the wood is winds,
in the holding form, in the seeking, in the branching of it;
the centre of the light
coming out of winter fields and walls that have lost their place
and ancient villages that have returned to earth.

11.

At Easter, on the seeking shore,
those with necessary prayers
and bells in the head,
pilgrims seeking
their child of light.

David H W Grubb

NEW ISLANDS

at the third turn of an echo
the encore begins   we will be more
together   give or take   than there was
something to do with speaking into the future

near the beach   exchanging
with tides to light and shade
glossing over specifics   bottles
a footprint   rounded plastic

dancers trained in moon enhancement
glide over craters ruffling their flags
to touch a decision taken
rock's malleable glands   lava overheard

Nathan Thompson

Of Eagles & Thermals

. . . and how to reach Upbeat, when the act of painting
filled him with dread. At Anticoli Corrado, across from the
Abruzzi mountains. The Thermal (s) there. On which, the
guide told me, eagles float, swooping down sometimes to
take a climber's dog. At 5000 feet we look up, anxious. The
guide a fan of Daniele Sepe who set 'La Montanara', that Alan
Lomax, Lanyon's contemporary in visiting Italy, recorded.
'La Montanara' . . . the aching folk laments of Abruzzo / the
mountain girls he drew and painted. At Corsham Court,
but bored with Wiltshire. & suffered from the voracious,
complicated void that is depression. Blue Day. Worked with
blowtorch, & pain, on assemblages, took to gliding, for sport
& to map a landscape. Overview & meeting. And to St Ives.
Porthmeor & Porthleven. Marine rust— the wreckage of a
sea. Surmise credits the era's fears . . . & gliding. Eagle to reach
Upbeat, & work it. Gliding, sustained minor injuries— but
died. And I try to explain field recordings to a mountain
guide whose language I cannot speak. And down from
Castelluccio to the bleak Piano Grande, burnt ochre from
long summer, the Paragliders descend. Starkly beautiful, but,
she says, you would go mad in the end, living here, & looking
at that view.

Stephen C Middleton

ALFRED WALLIS, PAINTER

On bellows, tea-chests, stoneware jars—
any surface that came to hand—

he painted sailing boats indoors
with tins of good ship's paint.

Well up on 'primitives'
Nicholson knew what to see

when he peered into the cottage
in 1928—

boats sliding off every plane,
perspective undiscovered,

the sky birdless, opaque,
like the cornea of God.

Boats toil on slopes of churning white
or black or grey-black waves,

beneath them giant fish-shaped fish—
'all the fish that God ever put in the sea'.

When there are human beings
they are diminutive

back-capped shadows,
facing the prow, harmonium music.

Raymond Friel

From Botallack Out

1

Where Hilton wakes restored
in the small acrylic fields of
fabulous women and dancing horses;
Celtic meadows, nocturnal and compact,
tip over the edge of the world
to raise a rampart of dreams
out into the Atlantic morning,
a white line under the door
he walks towards grinning.

For the pleasures of boats on the sea,
of returned desire, of animal breathing,
of abstract animate forms entangled
pouring through the windows,
jump up red dog, jump up:
what else have you got to do?
Your master's scraps fly from the table,
run in the blood of the living,
splash over the loving face.

The tone too is arranged by plan,
plains and contours, the simple colours
of the people's of the sea singing,
who will not let me sleep
rocking the sea all night long;
they ooh and ahh my secret acrobatics
as I cartwheel on the canvas of despair;
at different depths the light changes
aqua, marine, ultra and the green gods.

2

Q1
Is the text of your painting perception itself, so that we see the
work of the mind only in the act of painting?

A1
I thought when I was dead
I would not have to explain anything;
green branches shoot from my wrists
instruments of truth or nothing.
Horses caper at my back,
the tide of neuritis rises at night
cold and black licking at the gate:
text? text of what? paint?

Q2
Is it the layer of living things, through which other people and
things are first given to us?

A2
Layer of living things, that's good,
up to my elbows in that, paint,
bloody neck more like, Christ,
cat milk spilt bastard fridge broken.
My love the radio's on the blink,
will she ever tune to me again?
The signal's not clear, do nothing,
that record with Caruso singing.
I'm shipped up, skin flaking off
float me away in bloody bedroom,
the hidden life made apparent
free as painting the air blue, red,

vitamin B injections useless
first person lost down the lane boy I.

Q3
Are you conscious of the body as the unperceived term in the
centre towards which objects turn?

A3
No getting away from it is there,
especially when it rots raw umber,
nor pens that don't work, empty bottles,
Ronseal awash in the whisky ditch at 3.30 a.m.
fucking objects bite back all the time,
garlic, spinach, blue lake acrylic.
I saw the ghost body under the boat
at one with the waves, the fatal current
all my life, that face emerging:
it's all my fault, I am a shit.
The medicine,s a vicious circle,
I sailed around the cirkle islands
swapped pretty boy warbling
for Lord of All Things Moist,
ivy wrapped my every limb afloat.
I bear the young tree sprouting
in my craft or sullen barque,
good dog Spot
               got through another night.

Q4
So, in the sense that all thought is thought about something. . .?

A4
Afterthought I am, I found something
to paint about

writing *The Night Letters* the
for enjoyment, only for
something to do between pictures,
my figures come breaking out

light will break for another
creation and haddock breakfast
from Botallack out, my figures
left on the table for your edification

3

We came in after a swim,
the rain didn't fall and the sky
rose again into depthless blue,
Taygetus refocused and the temperature
climbed the bronze terraces for summer.

Inside I set up my Hilton gallery,
ripped open an A4 cardboard envelope
stuck three colour printer copies on it
and propped it on the chair,
Oi Yoi Yoi, two boats in the harbour.

A third, late gouache, half abstraction,
a brown eyed sun top left and
two blue figures dancing by the ochre band;

I think it's jungle music,
I think it's jig-a-jig time.

Sea-light across the square lifts
at the window, the heavy perfume
of white stephanotis butters the air;
each picture is a revelation
surrounded by torn cardboard.

What they say is unbearable,
beauty burning through our veins;
we wrapped it up for years,
the life that isn't life, a proxy framework,
full of holes and useless.

Look: rip open the envelope,
they spill out, splash and shout,
women and gods and boats
go charging around the house,
—Oi Yoi Yoi, there's a fire.

It snakes under the skin,
sways Arcadia and lifts the tide,
sends birds with messages tree to tree
singing all the names of fire
from the back of Hilton's cart.

Kelvin Corcoran

A Short Life of W S Graham

April on Rannoch Moor—
actual snow smothers
the print of weary nouns.

A fortunate bothie—
foxes saunter right in.

     ★

The bandwagon rolls past
on its road to nowhere—
Yer no Scottish enough!

Sydney and Two Roberts
thunder their approval.

     ★

Nightly over London
V-bombs and flying bombs
look for a place to land.

On the hike to Highgate
they send up metaphors.

     ★

Grey evening in Zennor—
nothing left of whisky,
paraffin or paper.

The radio exhales
melancholy numbers.

★

Not in imagery
or the lump in the throat
but an engineer's draft.

Not in observation
but the sound of the words.

★

In the warmth of his lair,
right arm of the poet
rests on his typewriter.

Upright in coastal light—
brow's corrugated frown.

★

In an evening of fame,
torpid with drink, his friends
steer him to the lectern.

'Am I a poet or
just a boy from Greenock?'

★

His shade comes to the bank
of Loch Thom—
                    NO FISHING
                    BY ORDER

chucks a fist of crumbs

                        to the reeds.

No public place for that head.

            ★

Out beyond the blue firth
and the bell's gentle strikes—

ocean's verbs   greyly shift.

Raymond Friel

CIRCULAR STUDY
for John Wells

Circles and the
shapes of circles not
exactly there
there perhaps suggested

a suggestion of circles faintly
drawn impressed imagined even

only half circled say half a

some time one edges ever over
slightly toward and into light-
ly one other not
one circle and another

some half circles

the shape of
lines
not there
        still
        seen

John Phillips

Five for Peter Lanyon

Mead Gallery, Coventry, January 1993 (revised 2009)

Construction for St. Just

The dead are laid cruciform on towers of glass. Bells form
radials, whose arachnid fault-lines mirror the street-plan.

Turquoise becomes transparency. Under the polished ground,
its oilskins prickle. Indolent lamps form hives. Chapels
crumble into the mist, as grey blood shivers in the space of
the clock.

Their wings are as small as the coracles of saints. Magnetic
lodes impale the ones who have plunged from solar heights.

Bojewan Farms

Woman, bent into the geographies of granite and moonlight,
sinks her face into the labyrinths of the west. A wave-horse
spreads its star-gazy dung across the tilth, where wind
sears rab with salt. Patience is painted as ancestral green.
Atmospheres retreat into her crimson tunnels. Riches are
displayed on the hems of clouds that, sailing *beneath* the soil,
anoint its bones with stars and verdigris.

Or, if you turn it over like a card . . . the skew-whiff patterns
of Brythonic settlements are revealed, lanes that evade the
piled-up walls for a beauty silvering the edge. Either way, you
must hold your ground—for there is no available ground. Just
layers of air, of area itself.

Colour Construction

Slivers of angels gasp in decompression chambers. Heavens
tighten in a gem made huge by clever photography.
At the core of this chunked-off form, a mine-stack's Set-black
shadow ascends. Desert prince, he is proud despite these stony
boundaries. Volcanic saps are doing their work—there is a
scarlet flash at each rampart of the base. Energy distends in a
feedback loop, as the brain implodes into a cell that mirrors it.
Atlantic midnight colours its edge.

Then light creates a sapphire alchemy. Rain takes shape in
mineral air. A white trace feathers at the chimney-top. Were it
smashed to pieces, this construction would become a deposit
of midnights, sleeked with batholithic downs in the eyes of
birds.

Soaring Flight

Blue takes off in bestiaries of thunder, sated with forms that
coerce repentance.

Offshore, the buoys are hidden as porpoises flash past the turn
of the headland. Movement inscribes a scarlet slash, at the risk
of a kistvaen chamber for the knights of vertigo. Here is one
propelling his helicopter horse, a whir of swifts beside him as
he swirls defencelessly. And the scene is crossed by a darker
trance—that is how one's dessicated life can appear, when
slicked in a seagull's eye.

Icarus is inscribed on sanguine wax. The way back down, and
the way back when, are rarely the same.

Glide Path

This one surmounts a cone whose occluded world is out
of focus. Twin tracks head across the August stubble-fires to
foam-quenched Polaris. The blood slick trawls its absence
over dripping fields too greasy to walk. The world below is
unfocussed, for your sweat has coated the lens. It dribbles from
wings. Kernow ceases to be real, its kobold beacons opaque and
mute.

Standing stones retreat into rusted shadows. The tribe's
mythologies are no longer able to save. A black fuzz at the
bottom left is in no way a premonition, but a beard of midnight
that looms like the Bay's leviathans. A paintbrush parts the
thermals, and the winds of applause can't keep you up.

Falling now, into the chessboard canvas of another county, at
the end of a summer joyed by play permutations, you have
nothing left to think, no way of saying anything more than you
already know. So you let your eyes re-create your childhood
landscape, hedging fields with stone and making them as
smooth as coal-dust, feeling rock stamp into your mind with
the shock of falling. Penwith granite fixes your gaze with all its
magnitudes.

You ignore the fall, the thump of a single pigment flooding
your mind, the death that is a razor slashing at canvas. Naked as
your birthday, you unravel into the silence of its crimson fabric.

Norman Jope

SCHOOLED

Late March, and pulling down
a branch with swollen buds,
red now, but closed up tight—
I find myself remembering

dozens of small clay objects
drying on the art room
window sill, echoes
of Hepworth, Gabo, Moore,

pictures of Bauhaus chairs,
Corbusier flats, pinned up
on cork-board, beside cloudscapes,
gull-wing Mercedes-Benz;

and, every now and then,
us being made to do
something old-fashioned as
a pencil drawing, maybe

of a jam jar full
of sticky-buds, the twigs
odd-angled, tipped with
ovoids, bursting green

most of us scratching, smudging
white cartridge, more than half bored
at the taut discipline
of how to look and see.

Tony Lucas

HOUSE AT MADRON FREE OF CHARGE
(For W S Graham on St Ives)

When something comes up like fixing the front door or thinking of a bathroom or buying clothes or doctoring my poor boy (I mean my cat who has gone and gone out of my poetry) we have little but I am able to put the Capitals at the beginnings of my lines and cook a good steak and kidney pie. (W S Graham, *The Observer*, 1978)

In the way that everything that becomes routine is recreated
Post-facta, after the gift, in a different moment in time
The life becomes lighter, light as a feather, you might say
And those days when I was living, working without a net
When I cut loose my feathers to flap free
And strut bravely widdershins, against the sun, to take the wind
Are now held up where importance had not washed over
For mimodramas parturition
It was a dacha after all, where the wind didn't blow
A retreat that gave birth to me
And I am after all a painter of restitutive patience
Working on a life free of charge
I am a believer of a different cloth
And with the Mother of Perpetual Help my patron saint
The picture venerated in the Church
The picture above the mantel
That came with the house, in the house that betrothed me
Like a friendship
The benefits of a gift of an artist friend
(Benefactors rarely come from within your own community)
But behold a man, a miserable sinner
Looking always, turning to Rome when he wakes
Bowing at thy feet—Destiny
Assist me for the love I have in me to give
And like a recommendation by me to you make me an angel
An indulgence of 100 days to be gained once a day

I never understood the expression
Or the full account of ennoblement
This house was to be
A found object
Reconverted, a holy estuary to you
And I am looking back
To set the scene once more

★

*Bryan Wynter's paintings also changed around 1956, losing their (albeit
indirect) references to the Cornish landscape and becoming 'a kind of visual
flux, a surface on which the eye found it difficult to rest so that, if it were
not rebuffed, it would be compelled to push deeper and come to terms with
the forces underlying the painting.* (qtd. Ralph Pite, 'Abstract, Real and
Particular: Graham and Painting')

I have been given the opportunity to live in a certain person's
            house
Operating in their space, with their mind, with their ideas
I like thinking about where this will take me
What victories will ensue
What truth will be for being in their shoes

How long do I have to live in this house?
And house is undefined
The house of literature
The rudiments we erect together
Doing all and saying little
We erect over, take us over the uncertain parts
Impoverishment
The kindness that you've showed me is in myself is in yourself

What will it cost me?
—Refreshingly you
It's like a shaking down
Me becoming you
And that's all there is
What did you mean about doctoring your poor boy?
You are a homo sapiens first, arche before techne

Jason Rotstein

PETER LANYON,
CAMDEN/CORNWALL

These paintings,
assembled from offcuts
of wood and glass,
conjure the wind and waves
in all their wildness, yet

away from the arts centre
the constructions seem
as small as we are,
lost in this city where
art clusters in white rooms.

•

This fall of rain
and sea's wild spray
stain the town grey with light

reflected from a restless sky.
Colour's thrown in abandon,
poured over roof and wall.

Today in Cornwall
your paintings
come to mind.

•

I've never glided
but now know how it feels.

Clouds hang low
over this empty beach.

Rupert M Loydell

Relationships in space
& the tension between forms

1. Barbara Hepworth's 'Three Forms'

'. . . absorbed in the relationships in space . . .
as well as in the tensions between forms'

So there is past, present and future
So there is man, woman and relationship
So there is me and you

and then there is her.

The space between us now, in the café
rips. Is a rip-tide.

Below, in the gallery, all the things
that still remain unsaid
are safely packed away in perspex boxes.

2. Paul Feiler's 'Morvah Grey'

Slowly it begins
slowly an avalanche
slowly

you have time to register
that it is not, as you once thought,
white on white

instead there are gestures of carmine
ochre, umber, gunpowder grey
and cinder

you have time to register
before you realise it's him
before the weight of it tumbles
and you are whited out

3. Ben Nicholson's 'White Relief'

It is not clear what relief
this white might bring
here there is only space

and the silence
peculiar to mountains
after the avalanche has moved on.

4. Mary Martin's 'Spiral Movement'

I have no patience with this 'work of the month'
this squaring of the spiral

a movement carré
cutting edges dulled
and all fluidity flown

my stiff smile
as if everything's ok

5. *Tacita Dean*

The bird is dead.

The moving image
moves

and moves on.

6. *Kerstin Kartscher's room I*

Every night over the town
the sound of wings

they might be birds
or falling leaves

or maybe the sough of hope
bottoming out

the world is full of
lost found objects

7. *untitled*

What I would like is a room the colour of sunshine.

8. Kerstin Kartscher's room II

This is a tsunami

and she's attempting to net the ocean

9. Kerstin Kartscher's 'Private War'

When you have all you need
in this tiny camp
why bother leaving over the wire?

Outside there is just
noise
it is in here that the war rages.

10. untitled

The bell-jar
keeps its secrets.

Roselle Angwin

No Snow

For Ben Nicholson

One line encounters the next
brushed with oil:
                    on top of diluted colour
the soft pencilling like sleet
                          at an alarming angle
with hilled horizons,
                solemn waves
and so much else
              like white water
mistaken for moonlight.

              There was no more snow today,
only your white

inside and outside the frame

              bearing what was hoped for
              in pristine order:

              glimpses, as if the past
              could be somehow relived.

Back at the old harbour wall
I waited awhile
              in the white ocean light:
how the tongue will remember
                    the sharp taste of salt
when naïve at twenty
              I saw on the chalkiest of blues

your childish red boats
in paint as dry as plaster

but shining like the surf
with the same sense

of stylish ease.

There was no more snow today,
only your pearl grey on white

that is pictured in front of me;

as if the slow pace
of colourless memory

avoids turning the world
into the darkest possible blue.

Peter Gillies

THE WHOLE OF THE TOWN

A view of St. Ives

Every cell behind your eyes tells you
all the roofs are not only itching
at yellow but have actually turned that,
as the whole of the town looks the picture

of possibility, framing itself in light.

In Fore Street, the house-tops are fields, valleys, hills,
The Digey, the quickest way to step straight out
of a gift-shop into the Atlantic, as the beach
at midnight wears the cold inside a fisherman's coat.
It gathers granite, windsurf, driftwood, a lot.

You'd think the waves would have got some kind of word
of marine blue by now but they never seem to;
as dots of sound in the harbour shift into sand,
circle around a wing circling a sphere.
Anyhow, that's the way I see it from here.

Phil Bowen

BIOGRAPHICAL NOTES

Roselle Angwin is a poet, author, painter, environmentalist and director of the *Fire in the Head* creative and reflective writing programme. Her work hinges on the connections between inner and outer landscapes, self and other, and creativity and wellbeing. She leads workshops throughout Europe in settings ranging from universities to islands, and is part of an occasional environmental arts group. Recent books are *Writing the Bright Moment* and *Looking for Icarus;* her novel *Imago* is forthcoming.

Phil Bowen was born in Liverpool in 1949, where he taught Drama until 1979. He became a writer in the early nineties. Work from his first full collection *Variety's Hammer* (Stride) was chosen for *The Forward Anthology* of 1998. He has also edited two anthologies for Stride—*Jewels & Binoculars*, poetry about Bob Dylan and *Things We Said Today*, poetry about the Beatles. His biography of the Mersey Poets, *A Gallery to Play to,* has recently been updated and re-published by Liverpool University Press. *Nowhere's Far—New and Selected Poems 1989–2008* was published by Salt in 2009. Since 1994 he has worked full time as a poet, performer and writer-in-education in over four hundred schools in more than thirty counties.

Kelvin Corcoran's work came to prominence with his first book *Robin Hood in the Dark Ages* in 1985. Eight subsequent collections have been enthusiastically received and his work has been anthologized in Britain and the USA. His *New and Selected Poems,* and *Backward Turning Sea* are both available from Shearsman Books.

Sally Crawford is a published poet and runs Poets of London (http://www.poetsoflondon.com/) and Westminster Writers (http://www.westminster.gov.uk/libraries/writers/mbnwriters.cfm). After training as a journalist she worked as a freelance book editor and now manages a social-science journal.

Raymond Friel was born in Greenock in 1963. After graduating from Glasgow University he moved to England and qualified as a teacher. His poetry collections include *Seeing the River* (1995),

Renfrewshire in Old Photographs (2000) and *Stations of the Heart* (2008). Ho co-edited the review *Southfields* and ran Southfields Press for a number of years. He currently co-edits *PS* with Richard Price. He lives in Somerset with his wife and three sons, and is the headteacher of a secondary school.

Peter Gillies is interested in the interaction of creative writing with the visual arts. Both a painter and a poet, Peter's work has been widely shown internationally: most recently in the exhibition *Zeit* at the Aspekte Galerie in the Gasteig, Munich (2008). He has completed artists projects at the Natural History Museum, London and Tate St. Ives. In Spring 2000 and Autumn 2004 he was artist-in-residence at the Scuola Internazionale di Grafica in Venice. His publications include *After Venice* (2002), *Sintesi* (2003) and *Passaggio* (2005).

John Gimblett was born in South Wales in 1960 and began writing in his teens. He is a teacher of children with S.E.N. and does occasional public readings of his poetry. His latest book is *Monkey—Selected India Poems* (Cinnamon Press, 2009) and he has recently finished writing a novel for older children as well as a crime novel for adults, based in Newport. He has travelled widely in India and southeast Asia. As well as writing and reviewing, he also paints and has a degree in the History and Philosophy of Art.

Geoffrey Godbert's *Collected Poems* appeared in 2008. He has 14 previous poetry collections. He is co-editor of two Faber poetry anthologies and is editor of an anthology of prose poems published by Stride. Harold Pinter said of his work: "Geoffrey will certainly end up with the poets in heaven."

David Grubb has a strong relationship with Cornwall and has written about it in fiction, poetry and his autobiography *Beneath The Visiting Moon*. His most recent volume of poetry was *The Man Who Spoke to Owls* (Shearsman Books, 2009). A novel set in the west country, and a collection of short stories, are currently seeking a publisher. He tutors in Creative Writing at Reading University, Norden Farm Arts Centre, the River and Rowing Museum, Henley-on-Thames and runs a mentoring scheme for individual writers.

Ursula Hurley teaches Creative Writing and English Literature at the University of Salford. Research interests include: nature poetry, innovation within prose fiction, generic distinctions between fiction and autobiography, and the pedagogy of writing skills. She is currently completing a doctorate, comprising a novel with critical discourses. She has recently contributed to *How to Write Fiction (and think about it)*, ed. Robert Graham (Palgrave, 2007) and *Everything You Need to Know About Creative Writing (but knowing isn't everything)* ed. Heather Leach and Robert Graham (Continuum, 2007). She was also the featured poet in the August 2007 edition of the journal *erbacce*.

Norman Jope was born in Plymouth, where he lives again after lengthy spells in other locations (most recently Swindon, Bristol and Budapest) and works at University College Plymouth St Mark & St John. His collection *For The Wedding-Guest* was published by Stride; *The Book of Bells and Candles*, a book-length sequence, was published by Waterloo Press in 2009, and *Dreams of the Caucasus* is forthcoming from Shearsman Books in 2010. Translation of work into Romanian is underway. His critical work has appeared in various magazines and webzines, and he also edited the literary/cultural magazine *Memes* and co-edited, with the late Ian Robinson, the anthology *In the Presence of Sharks: New Poetry from Plymouth* (Phlebas).

David Kennedy's recent publications include the collection *The Devil's Bookshop* (Salt Publishing, 2007) and critical studies of elegy and Douglas Dunn in, respectively, *The New Critical Idiom* and *Writers & Their Work*.

John Kinsella's most recent books include *Disclosed Poetics: Beyond Landscape and Lyricism* (Manchester University Press, 2007) and *Shades of the Sublime & Beautiful* (Picador, 2008). He is a Fellow of Churchill College, Cambridge, where the Hepworth in question is located.

Rupert Loydell is Senior Lecturer in English with Creative Writing at University College Falmouth, the editor of *Stride* and *With* magazines, and an abstract painter. His many books of poetry include *An Experiment in Navigation* and *Boombox*, both from Shearsman Books.

Tony Lucas lives in Southwark, but has been a regular visitor to the South-West over many years. He contributes regularly to *Ambit* and other magazines and has had collections published by Poetry Nottingham and Stride—mostly recently *Rufus at Ocean Beach* (Stride 1999, re-issued by Carmelyon 2009).

Stephen Middleton has had several books of poetry published, including *Worlds of Pain/Shades of Grace* (Poetry Salzburg) and *A Brave Light* (Stride). He has featured in five anthologies, including *The Stumbling Dance* (Stride) and *Paging Doctor Jazz* (Shoestring) with more to come. He edited *Ostinato*, a jazz/jazz-related poetry magazine, and The Tenormen Press, producing limited edition illustrated books of music related poetry. His live work includes readings, storytelling, performance pieces with musicians, and stand up comedy. He is currently working on projects (prose and poetry) involving jazz, blues, politics, folk art, mountain environments, and long-term illness.

William Oxley lives in Devon. His most recent collections of poetry are *Poems Antibes* (2006) and *Sunlight in a Champagne Glass* (2009), both from Rockingham Press. A study of his work, *The Romantic Imagination*, was published by Poetry Salzburg 2005. In 2000/1 William Oxley was poet-in-residence for Torbay, Devon, as part of the nationwide Year of the Artist scheme, and in 2008 he received the Torbay ArtsBase award for literature.

Brian Louis Pearce, poet and fiction writer, died in 2006. He was a careful craftsman who, to the end of his life, maintained a willingness to experiment both with ideas and with form. Music and modern art movements were among the sources of his inspiration and his many published works include the poetry collections *Gwen John Talking* and *Jack O'Lent* and the critically acclaimed novel *Victoria Hammersmith*. His final poetry collection, *Growling* came out in 2005.

John Phillips was born in St Ives. His publications include *Language Is* (Sardines Press), *Soundless* (Punch Press), *A Small Window* (Longhouse), *Pages* (CountryValley Press) and *Spell* (Kater Murr). He also edits *Hassle*.

Jason Rotstein is a Visiting Scholar at Massey College of the University of Toronto. He is Poetry Editor of the *Jewish Quarterly* in London.

Robert Sheppard's most recent book of poetry is *Warrant Error* (Shearsman Books, 2009). Other work is mainly collected in *Complete Twentieth Century Blues* (Salt Publishing, 2008). Also a critic, he has published *Iain Sinclair* (2007) and *The Salt Companion to Lee Harwood* (2007), and edited *The Door of Taldir,* the selected poems of Paul Evans for Shearsman Books (2009). He is Professor of Poetry and Poetics at Edge Hill University, and lives in Liverpool, where they also have a Tate Gallery, at which he read in the *Neon Highway* Credit Crunch reading in January 2009.

Penelope Shuttle was born near London but has lived in Cornwall since 1970. She is the widow of Peter Redgrove (1932–2003). Her most recent collection, *Redgrove's Wife* (Bloodaxe, 2006) was shortlisted for the Forward Prize, and for the T.S. Eliot Prize. Her work can be heard at the Poetry Archive website, and is available on CD. In October 2007 she visited Canada and the USA as one of three poets on a poetry reading tour sponsored by Arts Council England South West, *Cornish Poets in North America.* Her new collection, *Sandgrain and Hourglass,* is due from Bloodaxe in 2010. She is working on a memoir of her life with Peter Redgrove, *A Shared Solitude.*

Geoff Sutton was born in Scotland and used to be a teacher. Now he's grandparent, part-time gardener, hill-walker, reader of just about anything written, and occasional writer. Oh, and he's seriously addicted to Stoke City FC!

Sandra Tappenden was born in 1956, grew up in South East London, and moved to Devon aged fourteen, where she still lives. She has worked in dozens of roles that have nothing to do with literature, and a few that have, such as Creative Writing tutor at Exeter College of Further Education. A seasoned performer, she often collaborates with musicians and visual artists. Her collections include *Bags of Mostly Water* (Original Plus, 2003), and *Speed* (Salt Publishing, 2007).

Andrew Taylor is a Liverpool poet and co-editor of *erbacce* and erbacce-press. His latest collection, *Make Some Noise* comes from Original Plus and an e-book is forthcoming from Differentia Press. Previous collections include *Cathedral Poems* (Paula Brown Publishing), *Turn for Home* (The Brodie Press) and *And the Weary are at Rest* (Sunnyoutside Press). He has a PhD in Poetry and Poetics.

Philip Terry is Director of Creative Writing at the University of Essex, where he teaches a graduate course on Oulipian Practice. His work has been published in *Panurge, PN Review, Oasis, North American Review,* and *Onedit,* and his books include the lipogrammatic novel *The Book of Bachelors* (1999), the anthology of short stories *Ovid Metamorphosed* (2000), *Oulipoems* (2006), and *Fables of Aesop* (2006). His translation of Raymond Queneau's last book of poems, *Elementary Morality,* was selected by the *Daily Telegraph* as one of its poetry titles of the year in 2008.

Nathan Thompson grew up in Cornwall and studied music at the University of Exeter, where he later lectured part-time in musicology. He now lives and works in Jersey. His first collection, *the arboretum towards the beginning,* was published by Shearsman Books in 2008.

James Turner, recently-retired library assistant at Exeter University Library, has lived in Exeter most of his life. His collection of poems *Forgeries* was published by Original Plus. For five years he co-hosted Uncut Poets, Exeter's monthly poetry venue at the Exeter Phoenix Arts Centre. He enjoys walking, talking, eating, reading (mostly prose) and listening to classical music. His favourite writers are Dostoyevsky and Krishnamurti. Among his favourite composers are Beethoven, Malcolm Arnold and Purcell.

ACKNOWLEDGEMENTS AND COPYRIGHT DETAILS

Phil Bowen's 'The Whole of the Town' was commissioned by the Belgrave Gallery, St. Ives and previously appeared in *Starfly* (Stride, Exeter, 2004). Copyright © Phil Bowen, 2004.

Kelvin Corcoran's 'From Botallack Out' was first published in the version of 'Roger Hilton's Sugar' published in *Backward Turning Sea* (Shearsman Books, Exeter, 2008). Copyright © Kelvin Corcoran, 2008.

Raymond Friel's 'Alfred Wallis, Painter' was first published in *The Times Literary Supplement*. 'A Short Life of W S Graham' was first published in *Northwords*. Both poems appear in his book *Stations of the Heart* (Salt Publishing, Cambridge, 2008). Copyright © Raymond Friel, 2008.

Ursula Hurley offers thanks to Andrew Taylor, fellow explorer of gaps and gardens.

Norman Jope's 'Five for Peter Lanyon' was published, in an earlier version, in *For The Wedding-Guest* (Stride, Exeter, 1997). Copyright © Norman Jope, 1997, 2010.

Rupert M Loydell's 'The Barbara Hepworth Museum' was previously published in *Fill These Days* (Stride, 1990) and *Hepworth. A Celebration* (Westwords, Plymouth, 1992). Copyright © Rupert M Loydell, 1990. 'Peter Lanyon, Camden/Cornwall' was previously published in *Timbers Across the Sun* (University of Salzburg Press, Salzburg, 1993). Copyright © Rupert M Loydell, 1993.

William Oxley's 'Some Irregularics for Barbara Hepworth' was previously published in *Hepworth. A Celebration* (Westwords, 1992). Copyright © William Oxley, 1992.

Brian Louis Pearce's 'St. Ives Conjunction' was previously published in *Hepworth. A Celebration* (Westwords, 1992) and *The Proper Fuss* (University of Salzburg Press, 1996). Copyright © Brian Louis Pearce, 1992, 1996. The poems are reprinted here by permission of the author's estate.

John Phillips' 'Circular Study' was first published in *Poetry Salzburg Review*.

Penelope Shuttle's poem was commissioned by the Tate Etc for their website as a Poem of the Month. Copyright © Penelope Shuttle, 2007.

James Turner's 'Contexts' uses some information, and a couple of phrases, from *Barbara Hepworth, a Life of Forms*, by Sally Festing (Penguin, 1996).

Lightning Source UK Ltd.
Milton Keynes UK
08 April 2011

170611UK00001B/41/P